TEPUNG
GANDUM

BABAS
SERBUK KARI DAGING PEDAS

T0332324

KRIM KELAPA

Sos
Cili

TAUFU LEMBUT
高級嫩滑豆

SERBUK
KUNYIT

TURMERIC POWDER

KICAP
MANIS

SWEET
SOY SAUCE

Light
Soy
Sauce

COFFEE

KOPI INSTAN

MILK

A VERY ASIAN
GUIDE TO
MALAYSIAN AND
SINGAPOREAN FOOD

Written by **Shuli de la Fuente-Lau**
Illustrated by **Ann Jaafar**

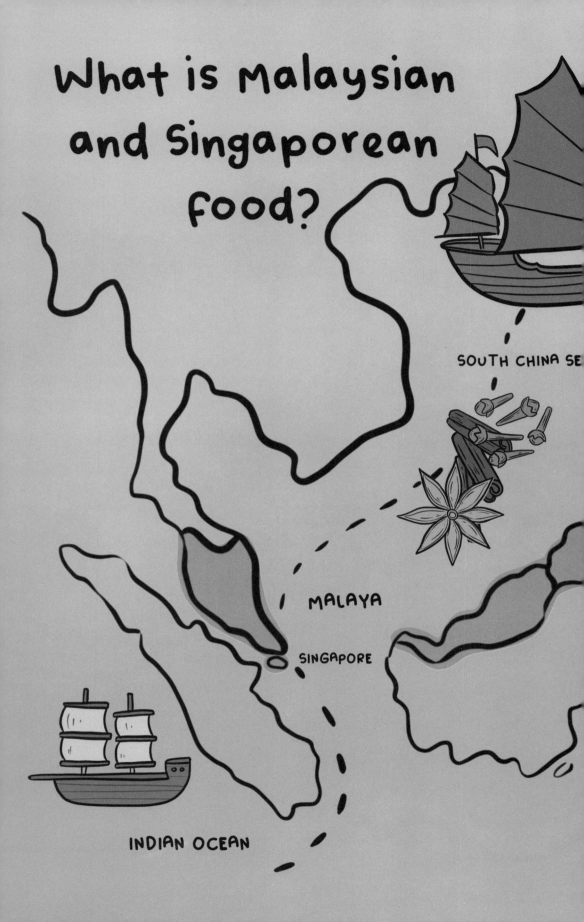

Did you know Malaysia and Singapore used to be one country called Malaya? Travelers often stopped by the different port cities as they were sailing on the maritime Silk Road, between the Indian Ocean and the South China Sea. For hundreds of years, people from all over the world would come to Malaya to trade.

Malaysia and Singapore are diverse Southeast Asian countries. With a wonderful mix of mainly Malay, Chinese, and Indian cultures, the food is immensely flavorful and unforgettable!

Because of centuries of shared history, both countries enjoy many of the same dishes—with some differences in flavors and ingredients. There is a friendly debate between Singaporeans and Malaysians about where dishes were invented and who makes them better. But no matter what, we all agree that food brings families and communities together.

Sudah makan?
Have you eaten?

KAYA TOAST (KAI-YAH TOHST)

Kaya toast is a beloved breakfast meal for kids and adults. Kaya is a creamy, sweet, and light coconut jam. Spread kaya over thick toasted bread with slices of cold butter to make this dish. Kaya toast is almost always served with a runny egg, seasoned with white pepper and soy sauce.

Adults like this breakfast with a cup of kopi, the Malay word for "coffee."

very

Comfort
-ing

Pandan is a plant used in Southeast Asian cooking to add flavor to dishes. Kaya is often flavored with pandan leaf, which adds a unique fragrant vanilla flavor. Pandan gives many desserts a green color.

Look for kaya toast at most kopitiams, or coffee shops. You can always find people eating and hanging out at kopitiams.

JAN
28

NASI LEMAK (NAH-SEE LUH-MUHK)

Nasi lemak is Malaysia's national dish. It is the perfect combination of many flavors and textures. This traditional dish includes pandan-flavored coconut rice, fried ikan bilis (small anchovies), egg, cucumber, peanuts, and sambal. It is often served with a side of fried chicken, rendang beef, or sambal squid.

Sambal, a kind of chili paste, is an important part of this dish. Sambal in Singapore is sweeter while Malaysians like it hot and spicy!

Very Fragrant

There are many different kinds of nasi lemak. Children sometimes eat nasi lemak with a fried hot dog!

Nasi lemak is traditionally wrapped with banana leaves and shaped into a pyramid. The heat from the food creates an aromatic banana leaf scent, so eating it tastes and smells heavenly.

HAINANESE CHICKEN RICE

Hainanese chicken rice is Singapore's national dish and is eaten any time of the day. Immigrants from Hainan, an island province in southern China, created Hainanese chicken rice. It is made with a few simple ingredients: rice, chicken, cucumber, chili sauce, and a side of broth. The rice is flavorful, the chicken is tender, and the side of cucumber has that perfect crunch.

Go to a hawker center, where hawkers, or food vendors, serve up delicious food. Each hawker specializes in just a few dishes, sometimes using very old family recipes. This means that the cooks get really good at making those few dishes.

Very Succulent

Count the chickens still hanging in the window of a hawker stall. If there aren't many left, you might not be able to get a plate of fresh chicken rice!

ROTI CANAI and ROTI PRATA
(ROHL-TEE CHUH-NAI and ROHL-TEE PRAH-TA)

Roti, an Indian flatbread, is a beloved part of Malaysian and Singaporean cuisine. It is called roti canai in Malaysia and roti prata in Singapore. It is fluffy, soft, and flaky, with crispy edges. It is usually served with dal or other types of curry.

Roti canai and roti prata were first made popular through mamak stalls, or open-air food stalls, in the region. Mamak stalls are run by the Indian Muslim community.

"Uncle" or "auntie" is a common way to warmly address anyone of an older generation, even if you're not actually related. In Malaysia, vendors and customers are often referred to as "boss."

It's fun to watch the roti uncle spin the disk of dough in the air.

Roti boom
(smaller roti made with sugar or margarine)

Roti telur
(roti with egg)

Roti bawang
(roti with onions)

Roti milo
(roti sprinkled with chocolate malt powder)

Very Fun

Roti tisu (thin, flaky roti sprinkled with sugar, and drizzled with condensed milk)

Roti pisang
(roti with bananas)

Roti is most fun when eaten with your hands!

Ipoh curry mee
(laksa with roasted pork belly or char siu)

Perlis

Kelantan

The Peranakan community is made up of people with Chinese-Malay ancestry. Their multicultural heritage influences many of the dishes of Malaysia and Singapore, as it combines different flavors and ingredients.

Kedah

Terengganu

Penang

Perak

Laksam
(laksa in cream gravy with rolled-flat noodles)

Pahang

Selangor

Kuala Lumpur

Assam laksa
(laksa with pineapple, cucumber, ginger torch flower, and mackerel fish)

Negeri Sembilan

Malacca

Johor

Singapore

Katong laksa
(laksa with short noodles)

LAKSA (LUHK-SAH)

Laksa is a noodle soup that is a true fusion of Malaysian and Singaporean flavors! Curry laksa is the most typical kind of laksa. It is made of rice noodles and a broth of rich, savory coconut milk and spices. This is topped with deep-fried tofu, egg, bean sprouts, a sambal chili, and either chicken or prawns and cockles.

Laksa is a Peranakan dish. It is a delicious combination of the history and diversity of the region.

Sabah

Sarawak

Sarawak laksa (laksa with thin rice noodles, fried egg, chicken, and prawns)

very

Rich

MEE GORENG (MEE GOH-RANG)

Mee goreng is a stir-fried noodle dish made with yellow noodles, vegetables, potatoes, tofu, and chicken or seafood. It is cooked in a sticky, spicy, sour, sweet, and savory sauce and served with a garnish of calamansi lime.

Macha, let's go makan and get mee goreng lah!

Macha means "brother-in-law" in Tamil, but it is used socially to mean "bro" or "fam," **makan** means "eat" in Malay, **mee** means "noodle" in Hokkien Chinese, **goreng** means "fried" in Malay, and **lah** is a word used for emphasis.

Manglish (Malaysian English) and Singlish (Singaporean English) use a wonderful blend of languages: Malay, Chinese dialects, Tamil, and English.

SATAY (SAH-TEH)

Anything cooked over a charcoal grill is hard to resist. One of the most beloved barbeque dishes is satay. This dish is made of skewers of chicken, beef, or mutton marinated with a rempah, a spice blend of lemongrass, turmeric, and shallot.

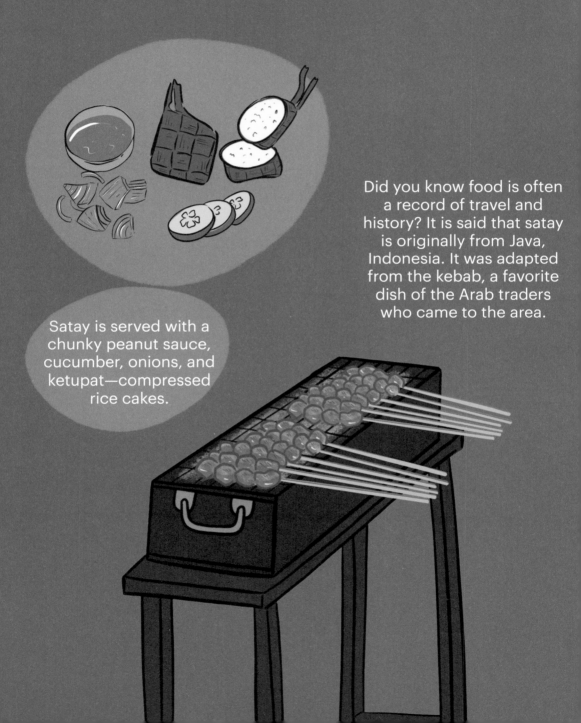

Did you know food is often a record of travel and history? It is said that satay is originally from Java, Indonesia. It was adapted from the kebab, a favorite dish of the Arab traders who came to the area.

Satay is served with a chunky peanut sauce, cucumber, onions, and ketupat—compressed rice cakes.

Very Smoky

While satay is cooking, it is brushed many times with lemongrass-infused oil and rotated often so there is char on all sides. The charcoal is fanned to make sure the fire stays ablaze.

Other grilled dishes include ikan bakar (grilled fish and seafood), otak-otak (ground spiced fish cooked in palm, coconut, or banana leaves), corn, or ayam percik (spiced chicken).

very **flaky**

The curry puff may have been inspired by British Cornish pastries, Portuguese empanadas, and Indian samosas. It is also known as karipap.

Epok-epok is a similar pastry, but you can see the difference in the pastry skin. Curry puffs usually have layered spiral crusts while epok-epok have smooth crusts.

hello! my name is epok-epok.

hi! i'm curry puff

CURRY PUFF

When you bite into a curry puff, get ready for a mouthful of delightful buttery flakes. Inside the flaky pastry, curry puffs can have different fillings. The most typical is a curried ground meat and potato mixture. You can also find curry puffs filled with vegetables, spicy sardines, yam, or a hard-boiled egg.

Today, curry puffs can be filled with red bean, durian (a spiky fruit), and even custard!

KARIPAP DAN EPOK-EPOK

PANAS

Curry puffs are usually deep-fried, giving them an all-around golden color. They can also be baked.

Kuih tart nenas are filled with pineapple jam.

Onde onde are covered in shredded coconut with gula melaka (palm sugar) syrup inside.

Kuih kosui come in two flavors: pandan green or gula melaka brown with grated coconut on top.

Kuih lapis have many layers.

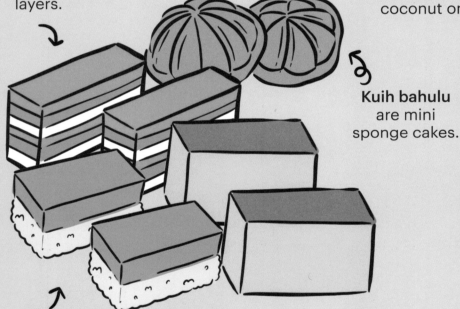

Kuih bahulu are mini sponge cakes.

Kuih salat have sweet pandan custard on top and salted coconut on the bottom. It is also known as kuih seri muka or kuih talam.

Kuih bingka ubi are made from grated cassava.

Kuih dadar / ketayap are pandan crepes with grated coconut and palm sugar.

KUIH (KWAY)

Is it a dessert? Is it a snack? Kuih is both! Colorful, bite-sized, and just a little sweet, kuih is wonderful to eat anytime. It's also perfect for parties, weddings, and festivals such as Hari Raya or Lunar New Year! Kuih is usually made with glutinous rice flour or coconut milk, and it can be steamed, baked, or fried.

Hari Raya means a grand day of rejoicing. It refers to Eid, the holiday at the end of Ramadan.

Kuih is spelled kueh in Singapore!

very squishy

Ang ku kuih also known as red tortoise cake has a mung bean paste filling.

MURUKKU (MOO-ROO-KOO)

Murukku is a crunchy, spiral-shaped snack. Dough is gently squeezed out of a press into a coil shape and then slowly deep-fried until it is golden brown. Murukku is an iconic snack during Deepvali, the South Asian holiday of lights that is also called Diwali. You will often find a jar of murukku during Chinese New Year, Hari Raya (Eid), and Christmas celebrations. It is also a favorite after-school snack for kids.

Murukku originates from the state Tamil Nadu in south India. It means "twisted" in Tamil.

Murukku can come in many different shapes. Even though it is most often a spiral shape, it can also be made into a ribbon or a rose shape.

It is made from rice flour and black gram lentil flour. It is seasoned with spices such as salt, crushed peppers, black pepper, asafoetida, roasted cumin, and carom seeds. Full of flavor, it is crunchier than chips!

Very crunchy

ICE KACANG and CENDOL
(AIS KAH-CHUNG and CHEN-DOH)

Most days in Malaysia and Singapore are hot! A bowl of shaved ice often hits the spot. Ice kacang is a colorful combination of sweetness and chewiness. Each bite is full of surprises like sweet creamed corn, red beans, grass jelly, and attap chee (palm fruit). This dessert is drizzled with condensed or evaporated milk and rose and sarsi syrup for flavor and sweetness.

For something simpler but just as sweet, try cendol! This is a shaved ice dessert with green rice flour jelly, coconut milk, red beans, and palm sugar syrup—simply delightful. Across Southeast Asia, there are many desserts that resemble cendol. Have you had Vietnamese chè bánh lọt, Burmese mont let saung, or Thai lot chong nam kathi?

Sarsi is a soda common in Southeast Asia and tastes kind of like root beer. A little sarsi syrup is drizzled on ice kacang, along with rose syrup, to give the dessert a distinct taste.

Ice kacang is also often known as ABC, ais batu campur, which means "mixed ice" in Malay.

Gula melaka, or palm sugar, is made from the flower buds of the coconut tree. It is thick, very sweet, and originates from Melaka, Malaysia. It is used in many desserts.

very unique

RAMLY BURGER (RUHM-LEE BUR-GUR)

Juicy, flavorful, and one-of-a-kind, the Ramly Burger is quite the experience. It always has a meat patty wrapped in a thin egg omelet, but you can add other toppings too. Sometimes called the Pasar Malam Burger, the Ramly Burger is a favorite amongst locals.

The Ramly Burger patty is halal and made out of beef. Halal foods are foods that Muslims can eat. Islam is the main religion in Malaysia and the third-largest religion in Singapore. This dish originated in Malaysia, but you can now find them all over Southeast Asia, and they're making their way to the Middle East and East Asia.

A pasar malam is a night market. Streets are shut down so that vendors can set up. You can find all sorts of food, snacks, desserts, fruit, and sometimes even clothes, toys, and other knick-knacks! It is a fun time to be out and about in the cooler evening.

DRINKS

To beat the heat and humidity, Malaysians and Singaporeans turn to a wide variety of tasty drinks. From fresh fruit juices to iced drinks to an endless variety of kopis and tehs (coffees and teas), there's something for everyone!

Kopis and tehs are made in a variety of ways: iced or hot, with or without sugar, and with or without evaporated milk.

Teh tarik literally translates to "pulled tea." Tea makers pour a full cup from high above another so that foam forms in the tea when it lands with a splash.

VERY SATISFYING

Tropical fruits longan and lychee drinks

Iced milo is a chocolate-flavored malt drink.

Fresh coconut

Sweet soy milk with grass jelly is called soya cincau.

Air bandung has rose syrup and evaporated milk.

Sirap selasi has rose syrup and holy basil seeds.

Typical fruit juices are apple, orange, carrot, watermelon, mango, or dragonfruit.

Very BOLD

DURIAN (DUHR-EE-AN)

Durian is called the king of the fruits, and it's easy to see why. Once you get past its tough appearance (check out those spikes!), you'll find a custardy, sweet, and slightly bitter fruit like none other. Durian is wonderful on its own, and it's also often found in desserts.

First discovered in Borneo, durian is native to Malaysia and Indonesia. It is said that the best durian comes from trees that are at least 10 years old. The older the tree, the better the durian! Malaysian durian is eaten all across Asia.

The name durian comes from the Malay word "duri," which means thorn. Don't walk under a durian tree when this fruit is in season in case it falls on you!

Malaysian durian is known to be especially fragrant and creamy. It has also been described as pungent, custardy, rich, and intense!

Because of its strong smell, durian is often not allowed in hotels and on public transportation.

Can you imagine what durian tastes like?

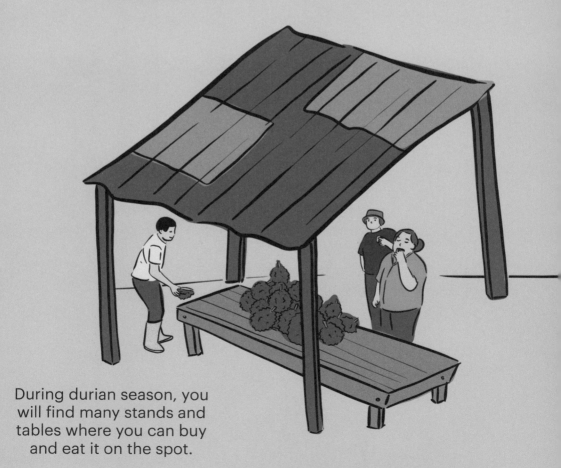

During durian season, you will find many stands and tables where you can buy and eat it on the spot.

Malaysian and Singaporean food has many different flavors. It is full of history and stories, and it's a beautiful snapshot of the goodness of diversity. Malaysians and Singaporeans are very passionate about their food! In fact, you could describe this love of food as gastronationalism—where food and its history promote and strengthen national identity.

Wherever you find a Malaysian or Singaporean, you will find a love for food and a love of sharing food. May you too find a love for the many flavors of Malaysian and Singaporean food!

I have special memories of my family making traditional Malaysian dishes while I was growing up in the United States. Whether it was the warm fragrance of pandan-infused coconut rice, the sizzling of little anchovies for sambal, or my father's attempt at making homemade kaya, our tie to our motherland was through food.

My childhood visits to my hometown Kuala Lumpur, Malaysia were full of delicious eats. As an adult, I'm fortunate to have lived in Penang, Malaysia, the food capital of the region, and in Singapore. Seeing my own kids delight in food that feels like home is one of my favorite things in the world. May you enjoy making these recipes with your grown-ups!

Sedap! 好吃! **சுவையான**!

– Shuli

Kaya Toast & Half-Boiled Egg

Ingredients:

- 200 ml coconut cream
- 4 egg yolks
- 4-8 pandan leaves or 1 teaspoon pandan essence
- ¼ cup white sugar
- ¼ cup palm sugar (gula melaka), finely chopped, or coconut sugar

Directions:

1. Separate the egg yolks from the whites very carefully. Run the egg yolks through a sieve to make sure there are no egg whites. Beat the yolks with a whisk or fork until smooth. Pour through a sieve again. Set aside.
2. Blend 4-8 pandan leaves (the more leaves, the greener the color!) with ¼ cup of coconut cream in a blender until the leaves are thoroughly blended. Add 1 tablespoon of water, if the mixture is too thick. If using pandan essence, skip this step.
3. Combine the white sugar, palm sugar (or coconut sugar), the pandan coconut mix (or pandan essence), and the rest of the coconut cream into a small pot. Cook over medium heat, stirring constantly with a spatula or spoon, until the mixture starts to simmer gently. Turn off the heat.
4. While stirring, slowly pour half of the egg yolks into the coconut cream mixture. Once mixed, pour the rest of the egg yolks into the pot.
5. Over medium heat, stir the mixture constantly until it is slightly thickened. Reduce the heat to low, and keep stirring until the mixture is thick enough to coat all sides of the pot and is a spreadable consistency. This will take about 8-10 minutes.
6. Turn off the heat, and transfer the kaya to a bottle or jar. Let it cool completely. Cover and refrigerate. The kaya will keep in the refrigerator for about one week.
7. Slather kaya generously on lightly toasted, thick white bread, and top with slices of salted butter, if desired. Serve alongside a half-boiled egg (pour boiling water over the egg in a bowl and cover for 7 minutes) drizzle with soy sauce and powder with white pepper for a kopitiam experience!

Saté Ayam (Chicken Satay)

Marinade ingredients:
- 6 shallots, roughly chopped
- 3 lemongrass stalks, roughly chopped
- 1 clove garlic
- 1 tablespoon coriander
- 2 tablespoons vegetable oil

Satay ingredients:
- 2 chicken legs and thighs, deboned and cut into 1-2 inch pieces
- 3 tablespoons sugar
- ½ teaspoon salt
- 1 teaspoon turmeric powder
- 1 lemongrass stalk, slightly bruised
- Skewers
- Vegetable oil

Directions:
1. Blend all of the marinade ingredients in a food processor or blender until smooth.
2. Combine the marinade paste with the chicken, sugar, salt, and turmeric powder, and marinate for up to 12 hours.
3. Soak the skewers in a dish of shallow water for 30 minutes.
4. Thread 4-5 pieces of meat onto each skewer.
5. Grill over a charcoal fire or grill. Make a brush by crushing some extra lemongrass and dipping it in oil, or use a brush dipped in lemongrass-infused oil; brush the chicken often.
6. Turn the skewers frequently to prevent burning. The satay is done when the meat is slightly charred on the outside and just cooked inside.

Sauce ingredients:
- 2 cups dry roasted peanuts without skin
- ⅓ cup oil
- 1 heaping tablespoon tamarind pulp, soaked in 4 tablespoons water, or 1 teaspoon tamarind powder mixed with 4 tablespoons water
- 1 cup water
- 1 tablespoon sugar
- Salt to taste

Spice ingredients:
- 6-8 dried chilies, soaked in hot water (optional)
- 6 cloves garlic
- 3 shallots
- 4 lemongrass stalks
- 1 inch of galangal
- 2 tablespoons coriander
- 1 teaspoon cumin

Directions:
1. Crush the peanuts coarsely in a blender or with a large knife and set aside.
2. Chop all the spice ingredients and blend in a food processor or blender until fine.
3. Heat the oil, and when it's warm, fry the spice mixture together with tamarind pulp until fragrant, adding the water a little at a time.
4. Add the sugar, salt, and peanuts.
5. Mix thoroughly and set aside to cool.
6. Dip your chicken satay skewers in the sauce or pour it over the top, and enjoy!

To my Pa, for your boundless dreams and endless stories. Thanks for always believing in me.
– S.D.

To my loved ones, thank you for being the unwavering support system that fueled my creative journey in bringing this book to life.
To readers, this book is a celebration of my heritage, and I hope it inspires you to explore the culinary traditions of Malaysia and Singapore in a fun and creative way.
– A.J.

A Very Asian Guide to Malaysian and Singaporean Food is first published by Gloo Books 2024.
Written by Shuli de la Fuente-Lau
Ilustrated by Ann Jaafar
The illustrations in this book were rendered in a digital medium.
For more information or to order books, please visit www.gloobooks.com or contact us at contact@gloobooks.com.
Follow us at @gloobooks.

ISBN: 978-1-962351-03-4

Printed in China.